The Humanistic Initiative

The Humanistic Initiative:

Bridging the Gap Between Science, Scriptures, and The History of Humanity

The Search for Truth Beyond God, Dogma, and the Unknown Technology That Shaped the Human History

Written By William Bowden

The Humanistic Initiative: Bridging the Gap Between Science, Scriptures, and the History of Humanity.

Published by: Sovereignty Book Publishing

ISBN: 979-8-9938712-0-2

Library of Congress Control Number: 2025-923751

The information and theories presented in this work are based on the author's research and analytical comparisons of historical, archaeological, and scientific data. The goal is to stimulate thought and discussion and to establish a historically and logically superior framework for human progress.

The Humanistic Initiative:

A New Agenda for Humanity

Appendices

Select Bibliography (APA 7th Edition)

Dedicated

To the inquisitive mind of the child who first looked up at the stars and asked, " How and Why?"

And to my wife Misty, my children, and my grandchildren—for their unwavering foundation that bore the cost of this long, comparative journey. Your support and futures allowed the speculation to finally come to this conclusion.

"The whole problem with the world is that fools and fanatics are always so certain of themselves, and wiser people so full of doubts."— Bertrand Russell, Philosopher and Logician

Table of Contents

Prologue:

The Humanistic Initiative

For millennia, the history of humanity has been a short story: a sudden creation, a moral fall, and a painful, recent crawl toward civilization. We have been tethered to a timeline of roughly six thousand years, taught that the monumental structures we left behind—the pyramids of Giza, the precision cuts of Baalbek, the impossible stone walls of Peru—were built by simple faith, copper chisels, and brute force. This narrative, a fusion of theological history and reluctant archaeology, is the foundational lie that dictates our understanding of who we are.

I am not here to debate theology. I am here to present verifiable, measurable facts. As a professional grounded in advanced material science and engineering logistics, I assert that the contradictions in our past are too numerous and too severe to ignore. They demand that we abandon belief-driven certainty and adopt a simple, non-negotiable standard: The truth must be the explanation that is the most logically consistent with the available evidence.

The evidence is overwhelming: Our history has suffered a Double Collapse.

The Scientific Timeline Collapse: We possess fossil records that scientifically verify the existence of anatomically modern humans 315,000 years ago, a fact that immediately proves the 6,000-year timeline is off by hundreds of thousands of years.

The Engineering Collapse: The precision and scale of ancient megastructures—which we will examine using modern tooling metrics—demand technologies (such as high-speed cutting and atmospheric manipulation) that are beyond the documented capabilities of their supposed builders.

These two facts—Deep Time and Technological Degression—force a confrontation with a terrifying truth: The inconsistencies in our texts and monuments are not flaws; they are the intentional scars of redaction left by a deliberate effort to enforce Technological Amnesia following a global cataclysm.

This book is the mandate of the Humanistic Initiative: to strip away the veneer of myth, reclaim our heritage of advanced science, and look past the short story to our rightful place in the cosmos.

Introduction

The First Act of Consistency

For every person, civilization, or cosmos, the inquiry into origins is the most essential act of self-definition. Our response to that question determines our morality, our technological ambition, and our collective destiny. Yet, for millennia, we have allowed this fundamental inquiry to be governed by comfort rather than consistency.

We were given a story that was singular, brief, and absolute. The Humanistic Initiative begins not with an artifact or a text, but with a foundational premise: The truth must be reconciled with every verifiable fact. The chapters that follow trace the inevitable trajectory of intellectual liberation. We will demonstrate, using the irrefutable evidence of archaeology, engineering, and cosmology, that the conventional timeline is a political fabrication system designed to enforce Technological Amnesia and halt the natural development of our species.

We will systematically dissolve the narrative of the "primitive man" and replace it with the portrait of an intelligent species whose progress was merely managed and restrained. This is an invitation to perform the first, most difficult act of intellectual maturity: the willing suspension of ingrained belief. It is a commitment to the Scientific Answer wherever the Supernatural Answer fails to account for the evidence. Our journey requires courage, not of faith, but of logic. The evidence demands a conclusion that it is far grander, more complex, and ultimately more optimistic than the one we were taught. Let the inquiry begin

Chapter 1

The Timeline Collapse and the Two Non-Negotiable Facts

For centuries, the concept of Deep Time has been a matter of academic or theological debate. That debate ended with the discovery of the Jebel Irhoud skull in Morocco. This single, verifiable scientific finding provided the missing link: remains of anatomically modern Homo sapiens dated using Thermoluminescence (TL) and Electron Spin Resonance (ESR) methods to approximately 315,000 years ago.

This scientific fact is the greatest contradiction in recorded history. If modern humans existed 315,000 years ago, the conventional 6,000-year historical narrative is demonstrably and irrefutably off by 294,000 years. This is not a small margin of error; it is a Timeline Collapse. We must incorporate this deep-time reality into our chronology.

By reconciling the 315,000-year scientific fact with the corrected current year by adjusting for the error of Anno Domini of 4-7 years, we establish the true age of humanity: 315,000 Years (Irrefutable Science) + 2,032 Years (Adjusted Calendar) = 317,032 (TRE) The term **Timeline Reset Year (TRE)** will be used throughout this book to denote the corrected, scientifically anchored age of humanity. The year 2032 is used to account for the scholarly consensus of a 7-year error in the Dionysian Exiguus calculation of the original Anno Domini epoch, a small but necessary chronological reset. The suppression of this colossal timescale is the central mechanism of the Intellectual Suppression Field.

The Technological Degression: An Impossibility for Primitive Man The second non-negotiable fact concerns the physical world. The engineering feats of the ancient world cannot be explained by the tools we are told they possessed. When we apply the rigor of material science, the conventional story immediately fails: A soft copper chisel (Mohs 3) cannot cut hard granite (Mohs 7) with the microscopic precision seen in Egyptian sarcophagi. The physics is non-compliant. The logistical challenge of transporting the 1,000-ton Baalbek Trilithon using ropes and rolling logs is a functional impossibility that defies modern energy output calculations.

We are forced to choose between two narratives:

1. The Divine Answer: The structures were built by powerful, unseen hands or by primitive humans guided by inexplicable spiritual intervention (belief over evidence).
2. The Technological Answer: The structures were built by highly advanced entities (human or non-human) using unseen science—a technology that

was subsequently lost or suppressed (logical consistency).

The goal of this book is to follow the Technological Answer down the path of logical consistency. Crucially, we operate under the premise that definitive empirical proof for either a Divine Creator or an Extraterrestrial Agency is currently absent. In the following chapters, we will use the principles of engineering, material science, and textual analysis to prove that the world's most profound enigmas—from the historical acceptance of slavery to the biblical ages of the patriarchs—are not myths or miracles, but structural anomalies left behind by an external agency managing a long-term human development program. We will prove that the dominant 6,000-year narrative persists because it is the most effective tool for control.

Chapter 2:
The Tools of Deep Time

Scientific and Engineering Proof:

The foundation of the Humanistic Initiative is built not on philosophy or faith, but on the principles of logical consistency and material science. If the current historical narrative were a construction project, its blueprints would be immediately rejected by any competent engineer. The physics simply does not add up.

This chapter establishes the two non-negotiable scientific facts that shatter the 6,000-year timeline: the true age of humanity (317,032 TRE) and the physical evidence of Technological Degression. We will introduce the **Four Criteria of Impossibility**, the analytical framework used to prove that the world's most enduring megalithic structures could not have been built by the people or the tools we are told existed at the time.

SECTION I.

The Jericho Hypothesis and the True Age of Stone

The historical consensus—the one enforced by the Intellectual Suppression Field—insists that humanity progressed from crude hunter-gatherer societies to sophisticated builders only after the supposed biblical flood event, marking the beginning of the conventional timeline. This hypothesis is contradicted by the simplest, most fundamental archaeological facts.

As established in the Introduction, the Jebel Irhoud skull proves the existence of anatomically modern Homo sapiens 315,000 years ago, giving us our Timeline Reset Year (TRE) of 317,032. This is the irrefutable truth. Any historical narrative that begins later than this date is incomplete and misleading.

The Scientific Basis of Deep Time: Radiometric Dating

The age of the Jebel Irhoud skull, and countless other Deep Time artifacts, is not determined by speculation, but by the scientifically rigorous process of Radiometric Dating. This methodology is based on the constant, measurable decay of radioactive isotopes, providing a natural, immutable clock for the Earth's history. The two primary methods used to prove the age of Deep Time are:

1. Argon-Argon Dating (40Ar/39Ar): This method is essential for dating ancient volcanic stone and sediment layers, particularly those associated with key human artifacts. Measuring the decay of Potassium-40 into Argon-40 in the rock allows scientists to precisely calculate the immense time that has passed since the rock solidified.

This process provides a definitive, verifiable age for the geological layers that contain the earliest evidence of our past.

2. Radiocarbon Dating (C-14): While less effective for materials older than 50,000 years, Carbon-14 is the gold standard for dating more recent organic material. It measures the decay of the Carbon-14 isotope in once-living matter, allowing for highly precise dating of structures and organic remains, reinforcing the timeline of civilizations like Jericho that contradict the 6,000-year narrative.

These tools are not instruments of debate; they are instruments of measurement. They prove that the history of humanity is not six millennia, but 317,032 (TRE) years long.

Jericho: A Monument to Suppression

The city of Jericho serves as a perfect structural anomaly. It is the oldest continuously inhabited city on Earth, with evidence of advanced fortifications, including a massive stone tower and walls, dating back to approximately 8000 BCE (10,000 years ago). This predates the entire conventional timeline of civilization. The existence of a highly organized, stationary, and protected settlement with sophisticated stone engineering 6,000 years before the Biblical creation is a direct, measurable refutation of the established narrative. This single site forces us to confront a devastating fact: the official historical record deliberately skips over 294,000 years of potential human development, which must include a predecessor civilization that possessed the technology to build and manage such large, organized projects.

SECTION II.

The Four Criteria of Impossibility

To move beyond anecdotal observation and apply rigorous analysis to ancient construction, we must define the parameters that prove a task is functionally impossible without advanced technology. The evidence of Technological Degression—the inexplicable loss of complex skills and machinery—can be measured against these four criteria.

Criterion 1: Precision (The Mohs Hardness Paradox)

Precision refers to the accuracy and finish required for the structure. The conventional narrative claims that hard stone (like granite or basalt) was cut using copper or bronze tools. This is a material science absurdity. Copper/Bronze has a Mohs hardness rating of approximately 3.0. Granite, Quartz, and Basalt have a Mohs hardness rating of 6.0 to 7.0. You cannot cut a material with a softer material, yet we see structures with cuts, drill holes, and finishes that demand the hardness and speed of tungsten carbide or diamond-tipped tools. The micro-tolerance fitting of blocks in the

Giza casing stones, or the polygonal masonry at Saksayhuamán, which fit together so perfectly a single piece of paper cannot be inserted between them, demands high-speed, high-pressure ultrasonic or laser cutting technology. The logistics of tool failure alone refutes the primitive claim.

Criterion 2: Mass (The Logistical and Energy Paradox)

Mass refers to the sheer size of the largest stones used, demanding an impossible energy expenditure. The most famous example is the Baalbek Trilithon in Lebanon. The three largest stones weigh approximately 800 to 1,000 tons each. Moving an object of 1,000 tons requires immense, coordinated energy. Moving twenty times the weight of a 50-ton stone across uneven terrain without breaking the stone itself is a logistical and engineering impossibility without anti-gravity or sonic levitation technology.

Criterion 3: Location (The Topographical and Transportation Paradox)

Location refers to the distance and topography involved in moving the massive blocks from the quarry to the building site. The granite used in the Great Pyramid of Giza came from Aswan, over 500 miles away. The Olmec heads in Mesoamerica, some weighing 40 tons, were moved across swamps and jungles, yet the Olmec had no wheels and no documented transportation infrastructure. To claim that hundreds of thousands of multi-ton blocks were transported 500 miles over sand, then lifted 480 feet, with simple ropes and sleds is to ignore the fundamental physics of friction, drag, and energy loss. The Transportation Paradox proves that the civilization responsible had superior mastery of transportation methods that could neutralize gravity and friction.

Criterion 4: Time (The Man-Hour and Chronological Paradox)

Time refers to the man-hours required to complete the structures within the constrained time frame of the reigning political power. The Great Pyramid of Giza consists of approximately 2.3 million blocks. Assuming it was built in 20 years, this requires placing, leveling, and fitting a 2.5-ton block every three to five minutes, twenty-four hours a day, for 20 consecutive years. This calculation does not include quarrying, transportation, carving, or re-cutting failed blocks. This statistical impossibility is the simplest proof that the 6,000-year timeline is a historical fabrication. The time required for such an endeavor must be measured in centuries, not decades, or the building was achieved using highly accelerated, automated technology.

SECTION III.

Structural Anomalies: The Proof of Lost Science

The application of the Four Criteria of Impossibility to global sites reveals that we are looking not at isolated examples of primitive genius, but at a shared, coordinated program of construction executed with advanced technology.

The L-Blocks of Peru

At Saksayhuamán and Ollantaytambo in Peru, we find colossal stones carved into precise **L-blocks, Z-blocks, and T-grooves**. These features are the hallmark of advanced construction designed to lock stones together against seismic activity. This is engineering, not masonry. Furthermore, the lack of tool marks on these perfectly cut and polished surfaces suggests a non-abrasive cutting process—perhaps high-energy sonic oscillation or plasma torch cutting—that vaporized the surrounding material, leaving no trace of the tool itself.

Egyptian Granitic Anomalies

In Egypt, the hard granite obelisks and the interior structures of the pyramids show unmistakable evidence of large-scale, high-speed rotary drilling and tubular core drilling. The marks left in the granite are consistent with a drill head applying thousands of pounds of pressure per square inch at high velocity. The claim that this was achieved with copper tubes and sand is refuted by basic engineering stress analysis; the copper would have failed immediately. These are not primitive drill holes; they are technological signatures of a lost industrial capacity.

SECTION IV.

The Logical Imperative

The existence of a civilization 315,000 years ago, coupled with physical structures that defy the known physics of the builders' supposed time, forces a single, logical conclusion: We are not living at the apex of human achievement, but in the technological aftermath of a collapsed predecessor civilization. The megastructures are not monuments to primitive faith; they are Structural Anomalies—physical signposts proving the existence of a highly advanced, coordinated global presence during our 317,032 (TRE) history. The ability to cut and move 1,000-ton granite blocks with microscopic precision is an engineering fact. The identity of the builders may be debated, but their advanced technology is not. This technological fact leaves us with two logically competing explanations for the External Agency:

1. A Divine power operating outside physics,

2. Or a highly advanced, non-human intelligence operating within a superior physics.

As neither are currently subject to empirical proof, the remainder of this book analyzes the historical and religious suppression field to determine which explanation offers the most consistent model for the human development program. The texts that govern the 6,000-year suppression field are next on the stand.

CHAPTER 3:
THE LOGICAL COLLAPSE

Timeline, Plurality, and the Crisis of Morality

The foundation of the suppression field we analyzed in Chapter One is not merely a denial of Deep Time, but a systemic Logical Collapse of the foundational narrative itself. For the current historical framework to hold, the texts that anchor it must possess absolute internal coherence. Yet, when subjected to critical analysis—when viewed not as scripture, but as an edited historical document—the Abrahamic texts immediately fracture along chronological, structural, and moral fault lines. This chapter systematically dismantles those fault lines, revealing a profound truth: the inconsistencies are not flaws, but scars of redaction that betray a history of external technological intervention and deliberate narrative control. The purpose of this chapter is to prove that the accepted timeline and monotheistic framework were strategically imposed to enforce a state of Technological Amnesia following a devastating global cataclysm, ensuring humanity never regains the knowledge of its **317,032** Year history.

SECTION I.

THE CHRONOLOGICAL FRAUD: DEEP TIME AND THE TIMELINE RESET

To accept the current Biblical, and historical paradigm, we must believe that all human history—all philosophy, all architecture, all civilization—occurred within the last six millennia. This is the central lie. By examining verifiable science and correct historical calculation, this foundational chronological premise collapses entirely.

The Clerical Error and the Seven-Year Lie

The starting point for the Western timeline, the BC/AD system, is demonstrably flawed. It was established by the monk Dionysius Exiguus in the 6th century and contains a known, fatal error: a calendar start that is at least seven years too late. This failure is not a matter of theological debate but historical and astronomical calculation. By reconciling the accepted historical death of King Herod (4 BC) with astronomical evidence for the Star of Bethlehem (c. 7 BC), historians confirm the accepted timeline is functionally incorrect. The true historical year is not **2025 AD**, but **2032 AD**. The reliance on a flawed, easily corrected human clerical error as the anchor for global chronology underscores the profound fragility of the entire official timeline. If the accepted foundation of time is based on such a simple, verifiable mistake, how can we trust the entire historical structure built upon it? It immediately forces a confrontation between the perceived truth and the measurable truth.

The Staggering Reality of the Timeline Reset Year (TRE)

The archaeological record **obliterates the biblical 6,000**-year window with **devastating finality**. The discovery of the Jebel Irhoud skull proves the existence of modern Homo sapiens **315,000** years ago. This is an undeniable, verifiable anthropological fact. This vast timescale must be reconciled with our corrected flow of time to establish the true age of human existence. The corrected, scientific age of humanity is calculated as:

> 315,000 Years (Jebel Irhoud) + 2032 Corrected Current Year = 317,032 (TRE)`

The correct chronological reality is the Timeline Reset Year (317,032 TRE). The suppression of this colossal timescale is essential to the post-cataclysmic control mechanism. By insisting on a recent creation, the ruling power chronologically collapses all prior advanced human history. Any artifact or megastructure that predates the narrative is instantly dismissed as fantasy or the work of primitive ignorance. This enforced chronological blindness is the most powerful tool of suppression, preventing the survivors from ever looking back to the true extent of their past knowledge.

Crucially, the knowledge of Deep Time was not universally suppressed; it was merely localized and contained within cultures independent of the Abrahamic narrative. The Mayan Long Count Calendar, which anchored time to a start date of **3114 BCE** and tracked vast time cycles, serves as undeniable proof. Its staggering mathematical complexity and cycles spanning tens of thousands of years demonstrate that a widespread, pre-Christian understanding of cosmic chronology existed. The fact that this vast, complex knowledge was deliberately superseded by the compressed, 6,000-year narrative is powerful evidence of a targeted, post-cataclysmic effort to enforce global amnesia. This was not a natural progression of faith; it was an act of intellectual warfare designed to simplify, restrict, and manage the psychological and historical memory of humanity.

SECTION II.

THE CRISIS OF PLURALITY AND THE CHANGING GOD

For the concept of an absolute, unchanging, singular Creator to hold, the texts that describe this deity must be perfectly consistent. When analyzed, however, the Abrahamic texts reveal structural anomalies and moral contradictions that betray a history of plural authority and managed iterative control.

The Plurality Paradox:

The Council of Creation

The most immediate challenge to monotheism appears in Genesis 1:26: "let US make man in OUR own image, after OUR own likeness." This is the most egregious textual scar. Theologically, the explanation of the Holy Trinity is anachronistic, emerging centuries later. Logically, the plural pronoun "US" implies a council, a group, or a collective authority was involved in the creation process—a theme perfectly consistent with the pantheons and "Star Beings" referenced in earlier civilizations (such as the Anunnaki of Sumeria). This plural reference is a remnant of an earlier, more scientifically or anthropologically accurate record that was later redacted to enforce a singular, monotheistic agenda. It is the text inadvertently confirming extraterrestrial intervention and a plurality of advanced entities.

The Moral Fault Line:

The Authorization of Chattel Slavery

The definitive proof that the foundational texts are a managed governance protocol and not the immutable word of a morally perfect being is their explicit authorization and regulation of chattel slavery. An omniscient, loving, and unchanging God would condemn the ownership of human life as an absolute evil. Instead, the legal frameworks in the Old Testament provide detailed instructions on how to acquire, manage, and inherit human beings as property. Leviticus 25:44-46 makes the distinction clear, separating the treatment of fellow Israelites from non-Israelites: "Both thy bondmen, and thy bondmaids, which thou shalt have, shall be of the heathen that are round about you; of them shall ye buy bondmen and bondmaids. Moreover, of the children of the strangers that do sojourn among you, of them shall ye buy, and of their families that are with you... and they shall be your possession. And ye shall take them as an inheritance for your children after you, to inherit them for a possession; they shall be your bondmen forever." Exodus 21:7 details the acceptable sale of a daughter into servitude: "And if a man sells his daughter to be a maidservant, she shall not be set free as the men servants are." These verses are not historical descriptions; they are legislative codes. They prove that the system prioritizes societal stability and economic compliance over universal human rights. The regulation of slavery is a moral contradiction that fundamentally undermines the entire claim of divine perfection and immutability. It is, instead, the signature of a superior agency that viewed the developing human population as a resource to be managed, controlled, and exploited within a rigid social hierarchy. Yet Clergy men and others still frame this with twisted narratives, while clearly reading the words SELL and SERVITUDE. The Bible clearly condoned slavery and selling of your own children. This is not a rule I can align with in any manner.

The Structural Scars:

Incest and Repopulation

The narrative contains unambiguous evidence of corrective and emergency management protocols. The command in **Genesis 1:28** to **REPLENISH** the Earth **("to fill again")** acts as a textual scar, betraying the truth of a lost, pre-existing civilization that was erased by a catastrophic event. This is compounded by the Incest and Population Paradox: if the human population multiplied from Adam and Eve, and later from Noah's family, then mandated acts of incest were required. The subsequent law against incest in **Leviticus 18** is an ultimate contradiction. The concept of an unchanging, omniscient divine creator is intellectually impossible if the creator requires an abomination to kickstart the very population He seeks to save. This points to a purposive cover-up, where the authors attempted to merge two conflicting records: the older, pragmatic records of repopulation and the newer, moralistic, control-focused laws required for long-term societal management.

The Late, Calculated Birth of YHWH

The concept of an eternal, singular creator is profoundly challenged by the archaeological record. The deity referred to as the father God in **Christianity** and **Judaism (YHWH)** does not appear in the verifiable historical record until thousands of years after the existence of modern Homo sapiens. While oral tradition places the Exodus and the start of the covenant around **1350 BCE**, the earliest non-biblical, written proof of the deity **(YHWH)** is the **Mesha Stele (or Moabite Stone)**, dated to approximately **840 BCE**. This defines the entire window of theological emergence: a maximum span of 500 years between its oral start and its written proof. This limited historical window, **315,000** years after the origin of humanity, confirms that the belief system is a historical and political invention—a calculated simplification designed to explain the overwhelming, lost science of the precursor civilization. This constant correction of protocols (changing reproductive laws, changing food laws, changing commandments) is not the behavior of an immutable God, but the behavior of a technologically or genetically superior agency managing a long-term development program.

SECTION III. THE FINAL EDIT:

REPACKAGING THE NARRATIVE FOR IMPERIAL CONTROL

The greatest proof that the Abrahamic religion is a managed control system is the fact that the entire narrative was drastically changed and rebranded to suit the geopolitical power structure of the emerging **Roman**

Empire. The transition from the Old Testament to the New Testament is the final, sweeping structural reset, proving that the faith's integrity was secondary to its global scalability and political compliance.

The Political Authorization of the New Testament

The New Testament was not simply "written;" it was canonized, selected, and formally authorized centuries after the events it describes. The process was driven not by divine inspiration but by imperial necessity. The Roman Emperor Constantine, seeking to unify his vast, crumbling empire under a single authority, championed the finalization of the Christian canon. The biblical texts were officially compiled and finalized at major church councils (such as the **Council of Nicaea in 325 AD**), where rival texts were burned and the political requirements of the Empire dictated which books would become the official narrative. The New Testament is therefore, a political and imperial document designed for widespread control and homogenization of culture across a massive territory.

The Calculated Change of Protocol:

Erasing Ancient Custom

If the Law was eternal, as claimed, why were the most fundamental tenets changed for the new faith? This reveals the engineering behind the control mechanism.

The Sabbath Shift: The Old Testament commands rest on the seventh day (Saturday). Christianity deliberately shifted the day of worship to the first day (Sunday). This was not a spiritual choice; it was a pragmatic alignment with the Roman Civil Calendar and the deeply entrenched worship of the **Sun (Dies Solis)**, immediately integrating the new faith into the Empire's structure and erasing a foundational custom that resisted assimilation.

The Invention of Christmas: The date of December 25th has no verifiable link to the birth of Jesus. It was strategically chosen to co-opt and replace the most popular existing pagan festivals: the Roman Saturnalia and the feast of the **Invincible Sun (Sol Invictus)**, which celebrated the Winter Solstice. This ensured masses of Roman citizens could transition to the new state religion without giving up their most beloved holidays.

These deliberate, calculated changes demonstrate that the Christian faith was meticulously re-engineered. The rigid, ethnically restricted Law (the **Old Operating System**) was replaced by a simplified, universally installable framework (the **New Operating System**) designed for imperial scale, compliance, and control.

SECTION IV.

THE LONGEVITY PARADOX AND GENETIC INTERVENTION

The lifespans recorded in the Bible pose a physical impossibility that can only be explained by genetic intervention. This anomaly is the ultimate evidence of a shared genetic history of intervention across disparate cultures.

The Nine-Century Human:

A Non-Human Genetic Component

Figures like **Methuselah** living for **969** years defies all known biology. This paradox is mirrored by the Sumerian King Lists, which record rulers living for impossibly prolonged periods before the Great Flood. After the cataclysm, both the Sumerian and biblical records show a sharp, dramatic decrease in lifespan. This strongly suggests that the long-lived figures were not simply "human," but possessed a non-human genetic component—genes introduced by the visiting extraterrestrial entities who possessed the advanced telomere technology to sustain life across multiple centuries.

The 120-Year Restriction:

A Societal Control Mechanism

This phenomenon is reinforced by **Genesis 6:3:** "My spirit shall not strive with man forever, for he is indeed flesh; yet his days shall be one hundred and twenty years." This is the key: the superior agency recognized that the accumulation of knowledge and power by an 800-year-old human posed a significant threat to their long-term dominance. An individual living for eight centuries accumulates institutional memory and the specialized knowledge needed to rebel against or surpass the celestial guides. The sudden, definitive reduction in human lifespan after the flood can be seen not as a divine curse, but as a deliberate genetic restriction imposed by the extraterrestrial entities. By shortening lifespans to just over a century, they simplified control and guaranteed a perpetual state of Technological Amnesia. The longevity paradox is the ultimate proof of managed human development.

CONCLUSION:

THE PURPOSE OF THE LOGICAL COLLAPSE

The inconsistencies within the foundational Abrahamic texts are not flaws; they are the intentional scars of redaction. The entire historical framework—from the flawed calendar to the managed morality and the shifted holy days—is a calculated effort to suppress the truth of

the **TRE 317,032**. The ultimate goal was to ensure
humanity, a species that once possessed the genetic
and technological capacity to challenge its
extraterrestrial builders, remains compliant,
manageable, and ignorant of its own vast history. The
final confirmation lies in the physical relics that survived
this chronological and moral collapse.

Chapter 4
Miracles, Technology, Divinity,

The contradictions within the foundational texts of humanity are not contained in a few disputed verses. They extend into the core biographies of religious figures, the physical objects that served as supposed instruments of God, and the very concepts of morality and time that govern modern civilization. When we confront the full weight of these discrepancies, we realize we are not questioning isolated stories; we are questioning a manufactured history designed to control and limit human potential.

The core premise of the Humanistic Initiative is this: If an event violates known physical laws, it is categorized as a miracle. If an event violates known technological limitations, it is categorized as a myth. The consistent recurrence of these "miracles" across history—many of which are demonstrably possible today through advanced physics—forces us to adopt a new classification: Miracles are simply Advanced Scientific Procedures provided by an external agency superior to the civilization receiving it.

SECTION I.

THE MORAL CRISIS OF LINEAGE AND GENETIC REMEDIATION

The concept of a perfect, unchanging God leading a moral society collapses when we examine the actions of His chosen figures and the nature of their creation. As Chapter Two established, (through the Longevity Paradox) the moral foundation of the biblical narrative is not a bedrock of divine law, but a rapidly evolving Governance Protocol necessary to correct the genetic and societal instability introduced by the interventionist entities.

The Noahic and Abrahamic Contradictions

The flood narrative of Noah—a story central to humanity's fresh start—becomes geologically untenable under scientific scrutiny. Geologists and archaeologists have confirmed a catastrophic flood around 10,000 years ago, aligning with a post-glacial melt event, but the indisputable fact remains that there has never been enough water on Earth to completely submerge all land and absorb that water instantly without trace (isostatic rebound, the lack of a universal sedimentary layer, etc.). This highlights a key problem: if the natural world cannot support the literal version of the story, then the event must be interpreted as either a localized phenomenon or, more plausibly, a highly selective cleansing event orchestrated by a highly advanced, external force using localized weather, geological, or atmospheric manipulation.

This failure of divine perfection is repeated in the moral lineage:

1. Abraham's Loyalty Test: Abraham, the purported father of nations, committed acts that the later, more developed moral code of the Bible would condemn adultery (having Ishmael while married to Sarah) and a willingness to commit infanticide (the sacrifice of Isaac), simply on the basis of an audible command. We should demand physical, verifiable proof before accepting the voice in one's head as divine instructions to commit murder. A perfect moral being does not ask for the ritualistic, terrifying murder of a child, but a superior, ethically ambiguous agency might conduct a loyalty and obedience test.

2.   The Incest Protocol: The lineage of Moses is rooted in incest. Moses was the son of Jochebed and Amram, a union between an aunt and her nephew. These close lineal ties were common after the cataclysm when the population was critically low, but they introduced severe genetic instability. Particularly a need for law changes throughout the Biblical teachings, particularly the

introduction of Levitical laws to prohibit these "atrocious acts," proves that an external force intervened, instructing humanity that direct reproduction through close lineal ties is dangerous and wrong.

This refutes the religious assertion that God is a perfect being who never changes His rules, forcing us to conclude that these rules were human-imposed necessities designed to correct earlier, genetically unstable protocols. This is not the work of theology; it is the work of Genetic Remediation.

SECTION II.

MOSES AND THE TECHNOLOGICAL MIRACLE

The story of Moses is not an account of divine magic; it is a clinical documentation of advanced engineering power. The events are not questioned in their existence, but in their alleged source.

The Parting of the Red Sea:

Atmospheric Anomaly and Engineered Precision.

The Biblical account mentions an angel, a dark cloud, and a strong wind. This phenomenon has two possible interpretations, both of which point to an external intelligence governing the event:

1. Natural Wind-Set down Theory: This theory posits that a sustained, massive storm—a "perfect storm"—could push the shallow waters of the Red Sea (likely at a lagoon or an inlet rather than the main channel) to one side, exposing the underlying seabed for a temporary escape. While scientifically plausible in theory, the probability of a storm with the exact directional force, intensity, and duration required to hold back a "wall" of water long enough for thousands of people to cross, only to collapse on their pursuers with perfect timing, strains the limits of natural coincidence.

2. Engineered Atmospheric Pressure Regulation: The alternative is that an external agency with the capability to manipulate weather or atmospheric pressure on a massive scale orchestrated the event. The physics required to sustain a wall of water demands an engineered, controlled application of force, not merely a perfect gust of wind. This event, accurately described as a scientific process, is best reframed as an act of atmospheric pressure regulation and localized weather modification. Whether achieved naturally or artificially, the uncanny precision, duration, and utility of the event—occurring at the exact moment of need and with lethal effect on the pursuing army—removes it from the realm of

coincidence and places it firmly in the category of a managed intervention.

The Wings of the Eagle:

Personal Transport Vehicle (PTV)

The account of God bringing Moses to Mount Sinai on the "wings of an eagle" (Exodus 19:3-4) is physically absurd if taken literally. The more logical, non-supernatural interpretation is that this "eagle" was a euphemism for a flying ancient spacecraft or a Personal Transport Vehicle (PTV). Moses did not ascend with an impossibly massive bird; he entered a craft and ascended with the external agent, whose fiery descent and presence were misconstrued as the all-consuming glory of the Lord. The smoke, fire, and shaking of the mountain were likely the side effects of a high-energy propulsion system or localized atmospheric heating upon landing and take-off.

The Stone Tablets: Advanced Plasma Ablation

After 40 days in the presence of the Lord, Moses returns with the massive, engraved stone tablets. We are faced with a crucial absence of proof: **The Ten Commandments' tablets have no verifiable physical existence; they are supported only by an oral tradition.** This immediately disqualifies them as a historical artifact, forcing the burden of proof entirely onto the narrative itself.

Beyond this lack of evidence, we face a profound logistical paradox based solely on the text's description: how could Moses have acquired, cut, and engraved these large stone shapes on a mountain with the primitive tools of the time without cracking or shattering them? This feat, much like the precision of the megaliths yet to be discussed, suggests the source of the commandments possessed advanced cutting and engraving technology far beyond human capability. The smooth, perfectly cut, and deeply engraved stone points toward the use of plasma cutters, laser ablation, or high-speed ultrasonic drilling, not bronze chisels. The tablets themselves—or at least their detailed description— The very description of the archival stone material may be an inadvertent acknowledgment by the external mentor that their protocol required a permanent, uneditable medium—a technological signature of a lost industrial capacity.

SECTION III.

THE MYTH OF MIRACLES: ARTIFACTS AS TECHNOLOGY

The most compelling argument for external intervention rests in the nature of the artifacts described in the **Bible**—objects that are presented as miracles but function demonstrably as powerful, highly dangerous devices.

The Ark of the Covenant:

Weaponized Electromagnetic Capacitor

The **Ark of the Covenant** is described in Exodus as a meticulously crafted, chest-like "device" built by Bezaleel under explicit instructions. It was not a storage box; it was a powerful, active machine. This amazing and elusive artifact was used to conquer Jericho, where its power supposedly brought the walls down. The possibility that this was a divine, magical device is no more valid than the proposal that it was an advanced energy device with an atomic strength or an undiscovered energy source.

The Ark, constructed of gold, wood, and topped with the elaborate Cherubim figures, functions as a highly sophisticated electromagnetic capacitor or a localized sonic resonator. Its power was not magical, but scientific. Uzzah's instantaneous death for simply touching the Ark **(Second Samuel Chapter 6)** is not a divine punishment; it is a clear symptom of exposure to extreme, unregulated energy or radiation that necessitated strict handling protocols.

The only logical conclusion is that the Ark was a powerful, possibly weaponized device that malfunctioned or was mishandled. The debate is compounded by its disappearance and final prohibition: in **Jeremiah 3:16**, God is said to have forbidden the Ark to be **REMEMBERED**.

This suggests a deliberate effort to erase the memory of an object that possessed a power too great or too revealing of the actual truth (advanced, non-human aid) to be left in the hands of developing humanity. This is further reinforced by the exclusion of texts like **2 Maccabees**, which claimed Jeremiah hid the Ark, demonstrating a clear editorial process designed to eliminate competing narratives and secure the technological artifact.

Aaron's Staff and Manna:

The Toolkit of Miracles.

The items stored within the Ark—Aaron's Staff, Manna, and the Ten Commandments—function as further proof of a highly advanced, external technology.

1. **Aaron's Staff:** The Staff was capable of being transformed into a snake, bringing forth plagues, and turning the Nile River to blood. This cannot be attributed to magic unless we wish to believe in the reality of witchcraft. The only realistic, non-supernatural explanation is that the Staff was a sophisticated piece of handheld technology capable of bio-manipulation (creating a snake), chemical manipulation (turning water to blood by introducing chemical agents), or focused energy projection (plagues). The fact that the technology was recalled (as evidenced by its disappearance) suggests a purposeful end to the intervention.

2. **Manna:** The food source that sustained the
    Israelites for 40 years, is described as appearing
    after the morning dew dried. This is not natural
    sustenance. This was a form of advanced
    nutritional technology, a Synthetic Nutritional
    Compound created with a device or process we
    have no knowledge of, deployed specifically for
    the outcast people in the desert of Paran. The
    total lack of similar substances appearing
    naturally since that time compels us to view
    Manna as a manufactured, artificial solution.

3. The Ten commandments which are the empirical
    prove that this deity exists with which without this
    artifact there is no proof and it has no factual
    basis in reality.

SECTION IV.

THE UNIFYING GLOBAL ANOMALIES

The case against any single religion being the absolute,
factual truth is overwhelming when we look at the sheer
diversity of global belief and the existence of hidden
celestial knowledge.

The Cosmic Calendar and Knowledge Suppression

When we examine the calendars that govern our lives, we find an unspoken, hidden cosmic alignment. Julius Caesar's adoption of the Julian calendar and Constantine's later elimination of the 8-day week in favor of the 7-day week align with this hidden cosmic rhythm. The 7-day week is astronomically arbitrary, creating constant calendrical chaos. The fact that an obvious calendrical system—a 13-month calendar with perfect 4-week months (13 x 28 = 364 days)—was never adopted suggests a deliberate omission of fundamental celestial knowledge from humanity.

The existence of a "cosmic calendar"—one based on consistent, natural astronomical cycles—is a piece of foundational knowledge that an external mentor would possess, but which a developing human civilization would easily discard or misinterpret. This is a subtle yet profound act of knowledge suppression.

Tibetan Buddhism and the Star Beings

The ultimate refutation of singular religious claims is found in faiths that achieve profound morality without a singular Creator God. Tibetan Buddhism provides one of the best examples. Adherents of this faith—whose nature is characterized by compassion, kindness, and docility—neither serve nor worship the Hebrew God.

Their belief system is founded on the cyclical nature of the soul (reincarnation) and an explicit concept that the soul moves on to an ultra-verse, continuing life with star beings in one of many possible galaxies and universes. This global phenomenon, where disparate faiths hold similar accounts of Star Beings and Giants (implying intervention and inter-species contact), suggests not a coincidence, but a shared, pluralistic historical event that was later localized and edited into separate religious narratives.

I propose that the theory of organized external intervention, when truly considered, could unify all these beliefs into a perspective that finally makes sense. Every religion is real within its own faith—a fragmented, localized, and ultimately misinterpreted account of an encounter with advanced, non-Earth entities whose goal was not spiritual salvation, but societal manipulation.

CONCLUSION: THE DEMAND FOR LOGICAL CONSISTENCY

Ultimately, the profound question becomes: What is literal fact? We must turn our gaze to the monumental structures of the ancient world. The forces that shaped ancient civilization never instructed humanity on how to move mountains or carve impossible monuments in the extant texts. Yet, today, with all our advanced technology, we often cannot replicate the very accomplishments of our distant ancestors.

This glaring discrepancy demands our intelligence. We, alone among Earth's creatures, possess a unique capacity for reasoning. We must use it now to look under every rock and search every anomaly. Can something be declared truth when we have never been able to empirically prove it? No. While many elements of religious teaching—an honest, humble life, treating others with decency—are universally wonderful traits, the spiritual foundation itself must be subjected to the same rigorous revision as engineering or medicine.

 We should stop waiting for divine intervention when there is no proof it has ever been here under the pretenses we have been taught and acknowledge that we do not have enough evidence or facts to definitively prove that either a singular God or simple unmanaged extraterrestrial beings are the true, final source of these mysteries. The truth lies in the undeniable existence of the superior technology, the necessity of the genetic correction, and the imposition of the resulting religious framework.

Chapter 5:
The Global Signposts

Engineering Beyond Primitive Thinking:

When we examine the monumental works of ancient civilizations, we are left with more questions than answers. The sheer scale, precision, and sophistication of these structures often defy the conventional understanding of the technologies and knowledge available to humanity at those times. These places, scattered across the globe, stand as silent, baffling testaments to a far more complex past than we are currently willing to admit. They are Global Signposts that point not to isolated geniuses, but to a shared, coordinated program of technological mentorship by an extinct precursor civilization.

SECTION I.

THE MERCURY ANOMALY:

GEOCHEMICAL KNOWLEDGE BEYOND CONTEXT

Teotihuacan, often translated as "The place where men become Gods," is a prime example of knowledge beyond context. This Mesoamerican site was home to massive, intricately built temples. Yet, incredibly, no definitive writing exists as to who precisely built these colossal structures, why they built them, or how.

One of the most intriguing discoveries within the chambers of the Pyramid of the Feathered Serpent was the presence of enormous amounts of liquid mercury. As a material and process design expert, I assert that extracting and handling mercury is a daunting and dangerous task. The inherent dangers of extraction—even minimal exposure can cause neurological damage and death—coupled with the precision needed to handle and store it, point to the fact that an unknown, advanced knowledge must have been imparted to these people.

Mercury is highly valued for its superconductivity and its essential use in electrical applications and the processing of noble metals (gold, silver). But how could these ancient people possess such specific chemical knowledge, and know how to extract it from cinnabar, without any recorded manufacturing methods or technology? The notion that they simply "trial-and-errored" their way to this knowledge is intellectually dishonest. This mysterious use of mercury is not isolated. In China, the tomb (Mausoleum) of **Qin Shi Huang,** the first imperial emperor, also contained pools and streams of liquid mercury, configured to represent rivers and seas. This mausoleum is clearly shaped like a truncated pyramid. This shared, highly dangerous knowledge of a rare, technically demanding substance points to a common, external source of instruction in the ancient past. The mercury was likely used not for decorative purposes, but as part of an extraordinarily complex engineered system—perhaps related to magnetic or energy manipulation, a core component of a power plant, or an engineered gate structure. The fact that such advanced, dangerous geochemical knowledge existed without any logical explanation in their recorded history strongly suggests the origin of instruction beyond primitive human thinking.

SECTION II.

PRECISION, EROSION, AND THE IMPOSSIBILITY OF PRIMITIVE TOOLS

The engineering feats at other global sites reinforce this picture of advanced technological ability. The problem is not simply how they moved the stones, or how they cut them. But why? What was their drive to perform such massive feats? This was all done before the inception or even the first ever known oral birth of the deity YWHW.

The Computational Complexity of Palenque

In Palenque, the Mayan city, the engineering defies simple explanation. How did the Maya gain the knowledge to perform such magnificent feats, using massive stones cut with incredible precision, often with inset coping cuts? These mortise-and-tenon joints and precision L-blocks are the hallmark of advanced construction meant to withstand geological activity, not primitive piling. The precision of these cuts often leaves no identifiable tool marks, suggesting a process involving high-speed oscillation or focused energy rather than simple abrasion. These stones are natural rock, not cast concrete, making the intricate, smooth cuts even more astonishing. The famous sarcophagus lid of Pakal, depicting him in what many interpret as a seated position within a technological cockpit interface, further fuels the questions about the nature of the knowledge imparted to this civilization—knowledge that allowed them to translate complex structural dynamics into stone.

Giza, the Sphinx, and High-Velocity Tooling

Egypt presents the ultimate paradox. Geologists have presented compelling arguments (like the water erosion patterns on the Sphinx) that suggest structures like the Sphinx may predate the last ice age, pushing the date back to over 12,000 years ago. Long before the, claimed 6,000-year birth of humanity. If true, this challenges conventional timelines and proves the existence of a far more ancient, sophisticated civilization than is currently acknowledged. Furthermore, the precision of the block fitting in the pyramids, along with unmistakable evidence of drill holes and saw marks in hard granite, seems far beyond primitive copper tools. These marks imply the use of high-speed rotary drills and saws, suggesting an ability to apply thousands of pounds of pressure per square inch at high velocity—a feat only achievable with non-primitive, exceptionally durable cutting heads. This had to be accomplished using some unknown technology, perhaps involving ultrasonic vibration or engineered plasmonic energy transfer, taught by an advanced source. "The practice of megalithic engineering disappeared from our capabilities precisely as the Abrahamic tradition became widespread. I assert this is not a coincidence; it is the defining chronological evidence that the new religious mandate was implemented to enforce Technological Amnesia."

Baalbek and the Trilithon: Mass and Gravitational Anomaly

Consider Baalbek, the mesmerizing collection of temples in Lebanon. While the Romans are credited with building the exquisite temples, they rest upon a foundation containing the Trilithon: three foundation stones weighing approximately 1,000 tons each. These are among the largest cut and moved stones in human history. To move a 1,000-ton block using primitive ropes, rollers, and human effort is a logistical and physical Anomaly. This scale of achievement points to the use of either:

1. Anti-gravitational or acoustic levitation technology taught the precursor civilization.
2. An organizational and material handling capability that fundamentally shatters the entire framework of classical history.

<h1 style="text-align:center">SECTION III.</h1>

<h1 style="text-align:center">THE ART OF THE IMPOSSIBLE SCALE: BUILDING FOR A CELESTIAL VIEWER</h1>

The mystery deepens when we turn to sites whose colossal constructions were designed not for the ground-level eye, but for a celestial viewer, suggesting communication or alignment with the external agency. Nazca Lines: The Aerial Blueprint and Computational Drafting South of Peru, etched into the arid Pampas de Jumana, are the Nazca Lines.

This vast collection of lines and figures presents the ultimate riddle of purpose. The geoglyphs are so massive and geometrically perfect that their true, coherent form can only be appreciated from high above, as if by an aerial observer. Why would a culture with no known flight technology dedicate centuries of monumental effort to creating art only fully viewable from the sky?

The construction itself is astonishing: many of the intricate animal figures are formed from a single, continuous, uninterrupted line—a feat of drafting precision that defies the idea of simple, primitive surveying using ropes and wooden stakes across vast, uneven terrain. This site is the ultimate physical proof of a culture with a technologically superior mentor that possessed aerial reconnaissance capabilities and passed down the necessary, sophisticated surveying knowledge—knowledge equivalent to a Computer-Aided Design (CAD) system. Even if these lines were used for irrigation purposes the question still remains, why and how did they use such shapes which they could not have appreciated themselves for no known purpose?

Poverty Point:

The Organizational Paradox and Non-Agricultural Control

Finally, we come to a site that offers a direct challenge to the established narrative: Poverty Point in Louisiana. This site is one I grew up around, it is one of the largest and oldest earthwork complexes in all of North America, dating back to 1700 to 1100 BCE. The monumental work required to build this site is baffling, with estimates suggesting that its creators moved up to 2 million cubic yards of earth—by hand. What makes this construction utterly surprising is that the Poverty Point culture was a hunter-gatherer society, not an agricultural one.

According to accepted historical models, only settled, farming civilizations with surplus labor should be capable of this kind of sustained, massive, coordinated engineering. The existence of Poverty Point shatters the conventional timeline of human societal development, proving that an external, non-agricultural organizational power was required to mobilize and sustain this massive engineering effort.

SECTION IV.

THE CHRONOLOGICAL ANCHOR: THE 12,000-YEAR INJECTION

The greatest indictment of the 6,000-year timeline comes from a single site that irrevocably proves the existence of complex, organized civilizations long before the agricultural revolution.

Göbekli Tepe:

The Dawn of Organized Complexity

Located in southeastern Türkiye, Göbekli Tepe is a megalithic complex dating back approximately 12,000 years (9,600 BCE). What makes this site a definitive Global Signpost is its context. It was constructed by hunter-gatherers before the invention of agriculture, metallurgy, or pottery—the supposed foundational elements of civilization. The site features massive, expertly carved T-shaped pillars arranged in complex, circular enclosures, often depicting animals and intricate symbols. This required: Organized Labor: Mobilizing hundreds of people to quarry, move, and erect 10-ton stone pillars. Specialized Knowledge: A sophisticated understanding of masonry and abstract symbolism.

Hierarchical Management:

The ability to sustain and direct such an effort for centuries, long before the invention of the societal structures that supposedly enable large-scale engineering. Göbekli Tepe is the definitive, physical proof that advanced knowledge and organizational capacity were injected into humanity at the very beginning of the post-cataclysmic era. It serves as the ultimate chronological anchor, destroying the biblical 6,000-year window and establishing the reality of the Timeline Reset Year (TRE 317,032).

CONCLUSION:

THE HUMANISTIC MANDATE FOR THE REDACTED TRUTH

The evidence from these locations constitutes irrefutable proof that ancient humanity was being taught and assisted by an advanced external source. This source was capable of: Genetic Modification (Implied by the need for incest laws). Weather and Energy Manipulation (Implied by the Red Sea and Ark of the Covenant). Mass-Energy Translation (Baalbek and Giza). Imposing Organizational Structure on non-agricultural societies (Poverty Point and Göbekli Tepe). The unified global evidence of advanced technology and organizational power is the Redacted Truth.

This truth demands a more complex explanation than either simple divine inspiration or unmanaged human genius. The evidence points to a shared, sophisticated, and ultimately controlling intervention that required the later religious movements to suppress the memory of its technological origins. The answers lie not just in the stars, but in the astounding facts right here on Earth.

Chapter 6:
The Plausibility Paradox

The Dogon, Deep Time, and the Inherited Celestial Curriculum

Our journey into the unexplained continues as we lift our gaze from the ancient stones of Earth to the distant celestial bodies that populate our universe. The more we learn about the cosmos, the more illogical it becomes to assume our planet is the sole crucible for intelligent life. The very elements and conditions believed necessary for life exist abundantly elsewhere, challenging our narrow definitions of where, and how, life can thrive. This introduces the **Plausibility Paradox:** How can we simultaneously accept the statistical immensity of the cosmos while limiting the source of our own technological, moral, and historical foundations to a single, Earth-bound origin story?

SECTION I.

THE STATISTICAL CERTAINTY OF COSMIC LIFE AND NOVEL CHEMISTRY

We must first break free of the primitive mindset that shackles us to geocentric thinking, embracing the very advanced scientific understandings we have gained since our known recorded existence.

Redefining the Habitable Zone

Take Titan, Saturn's largest moon. While it sits far outside what we consider the "Goldilocks Zone," Titan defies expectations. Its thick, opaque atmosphere, primarily composed of nitrogen, shrouds a world where liquid methane and ethane form vast rivers, lakes, and seas. Though not water-based, this unique chemistry opens up incredible possibilities for exotic life forms utilizing a methane solvent. The presence of complex organic molecules in its atmosphere and on its surface, along with evidence of cryovolcanic activity, suggests a dynamic environment where prebiotic chemistry could be actively occurring. This challenges the narrow, water-centric view of life and expands the probability of life elsewhere.

The Immensity of the Cosmic Ledger

The sheer scale of the universe provides the ultimate statistical argument against Earth's singularity:

1. There are estimated to be over 200 billion stars in the Milky Way Galaxy alone, spanning a diameter of roughly 100,000 light-years.
2. Current estimates suggest that every star hosts at least one or more planets, leading to the calculation of trillions of planets in the observable universe.
3. Given conservative statistical averages, astronomers estimate that hundreds of millions,

if not billions, of planets could lie within a habitable zone across the galaxy.

As a simple logical deduction: if someone does anything a thousand times, such as shooting a trick shot with a basketball, you are sure to repeat that shot exactly the same way more than once. Our Earth is only 4.54 billion years old in a universe that is a staggering 13.8 billion years old. That is more than three times our Earth's age! We, as a species, have gained highly advanced knowledge in a relatively short geological timeframe. Why wouldn't a race of beings, potentially billions of years older than us, possess knowledge and experience far beyond our current comprehension? The difficulty in accepting that an external source provided the technologies discussed in Chapters 3 and 4 is a failure of logic, not a defense of faith.

SECTION II.

INHERITED COSMIC DATA: THE SIRIUS PATTERN

Ancient civilizations, long before the invention of modern telescopes, watched distant star systems closely. This consistent, detailed, and technologically impossible astronomical knowledge is the most powerful evidence of inherited cosmic data—a shared celestial curriculum.

The Sirius A/B Paradox: Irrefutable Proof

The Sirius star system is comprised of two distinct stars: Sirius A (the brightest star in our night sky) and its faint, incredibly dense white dwarf companion, Sirius B. The existence of Sirius B is the perfect astronomical marker for an intervention:

1. Verifiable Fact: The star is invisible to the naked eye and difficult to observe even with early telescopes.
2. The Dogon Paradox: The Dogon people of Mali have possessed incredibly detailed and accurate knowledge of Sirius B's existence and its 50-year orbital period around Sirius A for centuries.

How could they have known this without advanced instrumentation, or direct instruction? The specific, verifiable astronomical data they possessed points to an undeniable fact: they were taught by a technologically advanced entity. We also know that Osiris, a pivotal Egyptian God, was prominently linked with the Sirius star system. This hypothesis moves beyond simple deification; it suggests these "Gods" were advanced refugees or technological migrants whose capabilities were simply interpreted as divinity by a primitive, receptive population.

Lyra and Cygnus: The Navigational Signposts

The Lyra star system and its brightest star, Vega, was a significant navigational and spiritual point for Greeks, Arabs, Romans, Mesopotamians, and Incas. Similarly, the Cygnus constellation, home to Deneb and the powerful black hole candidate Cygnus X-1, was watched closely across diverse cultures. What could have driven these civilizations to understand, chart, and even deify aspects of these distant systems, potentially as far back as 12,000 years BCE? This global fascination with distant, key astronomical systems cannot be accidental. It suggests a shared curriculum—a foundational layer of cosmic knowledge imparted by the external agency across the globe.

SECTION III.

THE UNRELIABLE COSMOS: ANOMALIES AND MAPPING FAILURE

The theory of advanced external intervention also provides logical answers for unexplained cosmic anomalies closer to home and underscores the fact that our understanding of even our own solar system is incomplete.

Mars: Catastrophe and Migration

Mars not only could have sustained life but absolutely presents compelling possibilities for past complex life. This planet shows compelling evidence that it once had a much thicker atmosphere and was definitely within the habitable zone. The existence of colossal structures like Valles Marineris—a canyon system spanning thousands of miles across its equator—fuels the debate: was this a product of slow geological processes or a massive, cataclysmic celestial event? If Mars lost its ability to sustain complex life, the migration of its inhabitants to Earth would be a logical and elegant explanation for the sudden technological injection seen in Chapters 3 and 4.

New Moons and the Incomplete Map

Our own neighborhood remains a mystery we are only beginning to map. The regular discovery of previously unknown objects proves the Solar System is not a closed book:

1. Jupiter's Undiscovered Irregulars: As of 2023, Jupiter is confirmed to have 95 moons, more than any other planet. Over a dozen of these were confirmed in the last two years alone, highlighting that even the massive, easily detectable moons of the largest planet were only recently added to the celestial census.
2. Saturn's Vast Family: Saturn holds the record with 146 confirmed moons. These recent additions,

many of which are tiny, irregular objects, underscore that our basic inventory of the solar system remains incomplete.

The fact that we are still adding significant data points to our solar system map makes it impossible to claim that we know the full history or gravitational architecture of the past.

The Unorthodox Hypothesis:

The Inner Planet Thought Experiment I have a wildly unconventional notion, a true thought experiment to push the boundaries of our understanding: what if there was another planet many thousands of years ago, positioned closer to the Sun than Mercury?

This highly speculative possibility, if true, could fundamentally shift the entire gravitational resonance of the inner solar system. Such a planet could have placed Earth, at that time, at the extreme cold end of what was then its own "Goldilocks Zone," aligning perfectly with the ancient ice age. If this planet were somehow pulled into the Sun or catastrophically destroyed, such an event prompts the question: could it have had a profound, long-term gravitational and energy-based influence that led to a gradual, universal shift of the planets to where they are today?

This scenario could lend a unique perspective to the idea that Venus could have actually been an Earth-like planet and quite possibly harbored intelligent life before our own planet did. This destructive event could be an explanation for where some of these external agents came from, at least from one possible source. We must exhaust all possible scenarios—no matter how unconventional or hypothetical—to even consider coming to the actual truth.

SECTION IV.

THE PATH TO THE REDACTED TRUTH

The existence of statistical possibilities for life across billions of worlds, coupled with the undeniable fact that ancient people possessed astronomical knowledge (Sirius B) that was technologically impossible for them to acquire on their own, forces us to reject the closed-system narrative taught by later, edited religious texts. The vast diversity of "Gods" in so many different parts of the world, all swearing allegiance to a being from the sky, is best explained not by a singular divine entity, but by pluralistic contact and migration from multiple advanced sources.

The resulting religious structures are a human attempt to organize and simplify a complex, highly technological history of intervention that was suppressed for societal control. We owe it to ourselves to shed unnecessary, restrictive information that provides no understanding, and instead, embrace what can and will add meaning and truth to our existence. We must not fear something that has thus far had no proof beyond people blindly following something that has historically driven nations apart. When we unite we are incredibly capable, and our only salvation is to salvage our morality and make the right choices. Fellowship is not only pertained to religion. Let us now explore some of the ancient and modern technologies we have proof of in the next chapter. Let us teleport our minds to these amazing realities!

Chapter 7:
The Managed Curriculum

Technological Prototypes, Prophetic Weapons, and the Engineered Gap

We have traversed the physical remnants of ancient genius, from the precision cuts of Palenque to the impossibly scaled earthworks of Poverty Point. Now, our focus must shift from the final product to the technological prototypes—the isolated remnants of knowledge that prove human civilization was operating under a managed curriculum of instruction. This curriculum was later aborted, leaving behind a massive, unnatural gap in our technological development. The core question is: How did we forget capabilities that now define our modernity, and why did this process lead to millennia of stagnation?

SECTION I.

THE PARADOX OF ANCIENT ENERGY AND CHEMICAL PROTOTYPES

The most compelling proof of deliberate instruction rests in artifacts that clearly function as sophisticated devices, yet stand-alone without any evolutionary predecessors or successors in the archaeological record.

The Dendera System: Plasma Physics and High-Voltage Discharge

Specific inscriptions in stone, particularly at the Temple of Hathor at Dendera, depict what looks remarkably like an elongated, self-contained light source—a modern electric discharge tube or a highly efficient plasma lamp. While conventional archaeology suggests this image represents a snake emerging from a lotus flower, this mythological interpretation fails to account for the detailed engineering elements: the base, clearly resembling an insulator or socket, and the cable running to a device that could be interpreted as a primitive generator or energy source.

For such a device to function, the Egyptians would have required a knowledge of plasma physics and reliable high-voltage static or pulsating power. The inherent contradiction between the primitive tools of the Egyptians and the conceptual depiction of controlled energy containment and transmission demands a technical rather than a mythological explanation. It suggests the external agency provided a working demonstration of power generation that humanity was unable to replicate on its own, until much later.

The Baghdad Battery: The Lost Industrial Process

The Parthian Battery, commonly dubbed the Baghdad Battery, dating as early as 250 BCE, consists of an outer ceramic case, a copper inner cylinder, and an iron rod. When analyzed from an engineering perspective, these components constitute the exact elements required to generate electrochemical potential (voltage) when filled with an electrolyte like vinegar.

The notion that this complex assembly was merely a scroll holder is a willful simplification. Its specific construction points toward a functional purpose, most likely electroplating—the process of using electricity to coat one metal with a thin layer of another. This process was formally re-invented in 1805 CE. The existence of a functional prototype capable of this advanced metallurgical technique two millennia earlier demonstrates that an advanced knowledge of electrochemical principles was available to the ancients, only to be entirely forgotten or deliberately suppressed. These artifacts were not the product of human trial-and-error; they were functional prototypes introduced by the external agency.

SECTION II.

WEAPONIZED INTERVENTION: THE ARK AND THE ATOMIC WAR

If the external agents possessed sophisticated technology, they were capable of both creation and destruction. The ancient Indian Sanskrit texts and the biblical accounts provide terrifying, detailed records of conflicts utilizing weaponry mirroring our most destructive modern systems.

The Ark of the Covenant: Directed Energy Weapon Analogs.

The sudden and lethal consequences of mishandling the Ark of the Covenant (as detailed in Chapter 3) are not an act of divine wrath, but the expected result of exposure to a powerful technological device.

- Uzzah's Instantaneous Death: The death of Uzzah (Second Samuel Chapter 6) for simply touching the Ark is perfectly consistent with exposure to catastrophic levels of microwave (RF) radiation or extreme low-frequency acoustic energy. Microwave exposure causes instant, severe internal tissue damage, organ failure, and heart stoppage—symptoms consistent with a sudden, invisible force. The Ark, being a complex golden vessel, functioned as a highly sophisticated energy capacitor or sonic resonator designed with strict handling protocols that Uzzah violated.

The Sanskrit Texts: Nuclear and Precision-Guided Weaponry.

The ancient Indian Sanskrit texts, the Mahabharata and the Ramayana, provide a terrifying, detailed record of an advanced conflict. The descriptions of celestial weapons

(Astras) transcend metaphors and become technical specifications for modern weapon systems:

1. **The Barbarika's Teen Baan:** Described as capable of marking its target and systematically destroying it, this is an accurate depiction of a modern satellite-guided cruise missile or a sophisticated smart munition with GPS/inertial guidance.
2. **The Brahmastra:** The ultimate weapon. Its described effects—"scorched earth," the death of crops, the hair and nails falling out of survivors, and the heat capable of incinerating legions—are scientifically indistinguishable from the catastrophic output of a thermonuclear (fusion) weapon.

The controversy surrounding global sites that contain extreme, inexplicable paleo-radiation forces us to question whether these texts are mythology or historical accounts of a war fought with atomic-level technology long before our modern understanding. The only rational conclusion is that the ancient conflicts were not between tribes wielding bronze, but between or among the advanced external agencies, and the resulting destruction and fear led directly to the subsequent imposition of the religious code to control the traumatized, technologically disarmed human population.

SECTION III.

BLUEPRINTS OF LOST SCIENCE: THE ABORTED CURRICULUM

The most powerful evidence of an intervention that was later withdrawn is the massive disparity in the human learning curve—the "Engineered Gap." Humanity possessed complex knowledge, yet remained static for millennia, only to suddenly achieve mastery in a geological instant (the last 300 years).

The Antikythera Mechanism: Lost Computational Science

Discovered in 1901, the Antikythera Mechanism is a hand-operated celestial calculator or orrery dating back some two thousand years. It contained 20 to 30 complex gears and is recognized as the world's first known analog computer. Its function relies on the principle of differential gearing—a mechanical concept so advanced that it was not seen again in Europe for over a thousand years. This object is not a one-off invention; it is a meticulously crafted, precise piece of industrial-grade equipment that implies the existence of a widespread, lost tradition of precision metalworking and astronomical engineering—a curriculum that vanished.

The Flight and Propulsion Paradox

Consider flight: ancient texts and myths speak of aerial transit as commonplace, yet humanity struggled for centuries to achieve it.

1. The Saqqara Bird: This artifact, dating to 200 BCE, possesses an aerodynamic profile with an aspect ratio and dihedral angle specifically designed for stable flight. could it have been an instructional aid or a model of a witnessed airframe, abandoned when the mentorship ended.

2. Modern Echoes: Element 115 (Moscovium): Consider the claims surrounding advanced propulsion using a compound of Element 115 for fuel and anti-gravity propulsion. The later, official synthesis of the element (Moscovium) provides a striking, modern parallel to the Dogon's knowledge of Sirius B. This pattern—esoteric knowledge regarding advanced energy and propulsion, once dismissed by the mainstream, later proving to have a verifiable scientific basis— is the defining characteristic of a managed information environment. The full, advanced knowledge of propulsion was the key component of the curriculum that was most aggressively suppressed.

The Superiority of Ancient Materials and
Engineering

1. **Roman Concrete and Self-Healing Materials:**
    The superior, durable nature of Roman Concrete,
    especially when submerged in seawater, is due to
    a precise chemical mixture involving volcanic ash
    that triggers a unique, self-healing reaction. The
    fact that we have lost the formula for a superior,
    ubiquitous construction material demonstrates a
    clear loss of advanced materials science that was
    likely part of the original managed curriculum.

2. **Acoustic Engineering and Megaliths:** The
    precision of the cuts at sites like Giza and
    Palenque implies a level of speed and material
    durability beyond primitive tools. This strongly
    suggests the use of focused acoustic resonance
    or ultrasonic vibration technology to weaken and
    cut stone—a science that would also explain the
    logistical impossibility of moving 1,000-ton blocks
    like the Baalbek Trilithon. We are left with an
    undeniable conclusion: the history of human
    technological achievement is not a continuous,
    gradual ascent, but a story of advanced
    instruction, a global conflict involving superior
    technology, and a subsequent, deliberate
    retraction of knowledge enforced by a powerful
    external agency. This retraction paved the way for
    the establishment of the simplified, controlling

religious narratives that dominate our current history. To find the truth, we must stop accepting the narrative of primitive man and embrace the irrefutable evidence of the Managed Curriculum.

Are you ready to continue our journey into the next chapter?

Chapter 8:
Converging Technologies:

Where Ancient Science Meets Modern Physics

The Two Timelines: Re-Acquisition of the Managed Curriculum

Chapter Six presented undeniable evidence that the human historical record is littered with functional prototypes—the Antikythera Mechanism, the Baghdad Battery, the Saqqara Bird—artifacts that prove an advanced technological curriculum was introduced and then aggressively withdrawn. The presence of these devices creates a massive, unnatural gap between the primitive man of 200 BCE and the hyper-advanced engineering they imply.

This chapter closes that gap. Our modern scientific pursuit is not a journey into the unknown; it is a meticulously documented, agonizingly slow re-acquisition of the advanced knowledge that was deliberately purged from our collective memory. We are not inventing. We are finally catching up to the lost science of the ancients. The true breakthrough is recognizing that the "miracles" of the ancient world are simply standard physics applied by a superior instruction set.

SECTION I.

THE ACOUSTIC-GRAVITATIONAL INTERFACE: SOUND AS THE MASTER TOOL

For millennia, the most complex construction feats—from the perfectly fitted polygonal walls of Cusco to the precision cuts of the Giza core stones—have been attributed to impossibly persistent slave labor using bronze tools. This explanation violates every principle of engineering and physics. The logical explanation must lie in the manipulation of materials using energy, specifically vibrational and sonic frequency to bypass the limits of mass.

Ancient Resonance Chambers and Material Manipulation

Many megalithic structures, including the Hypogeum in Malta and the great pyramids, are engineered not merely as tombs or monuments, but as resonance chambers. The stone walls and specific geometries enhance acoustic energy, achieving peak amplification at frequencies that can affect human consciousness and, critically, the molecular structure of matter. If a certain frequency can shatter a glass, a precisely targeted frequency can liquefy or manipulate the crystalline structure of granite.

- The Coral Castle Enigma: In the early 20th century, Edward Leedskalnin single-handedly quarried, moved, and erected megalithic stone blocks up to 30 tons to build Coral Castle in Florida. He claimed to know the secret to moving mass, attributing it to a knowledge of magnetic current and gravitational leverage. His claims align with the principles of the Hutchison Effect—an unexplained phenomenon involving the convergence of high-voltage static electricity, magnetic fields, and electromagnetic energy that can result in the levitation and anomalous dissolution of heavy materials. This suggests an intuitive or inherited understanding of zero-point energy manipulation through resonance.

Modern Sonic Metallurgy and NDT

Modern technology has confirmed the principle of sound as a tool, proving the scale of ancient engineering is now a solvable problem:

1. Ultrasonic Welding and Cutting: We use high-frequency ultrasonic energy to weld dissimilar metals, cut composite materials, and perform precise, non-contact surgery.
2. Sonochemistry: This field uses high-intensity ultrasound to speed up chemical reactions and even break down molecular bonds, demonstrating that vibration can utterly change material properties.
3. Non-Destructive Testing (NDT): Engineers use ultrasonic waves to detect flaws and measure

stress within concrete and metal, proving that sound interacts with and reveals the internal state of massive material structures.

The difference between the ancient and modern is scale, not principle. Ancient engineers understood the specific resonant frequency of stone and exploited it to move mountains; we are only now using the same principles in a controlled lab environment.

SECTION II.

PROPULSION AND MATERIALS: THE DIVERGENCE IN POWER SYSTEMS

The gap in power generation and transportation is perhaps the most glaring evidence of the Managed Curriculum's withdrawal. The key to this lost science is the manipulation of the fabric of spacetime, not just air resistance.

The Vedic Blueprint for Reactionless Flight

Ancient Indian texts provide sophisticated descriptions of Vimanas—mythological flying palaces or airships. The Sanskrit texts describe propulsion methods that sound remarkably like advanced physics:

1. Mercury Vortex Engines (MHD): Some Vimanas are described as being powered by a complex system involving mercury, a metal with high thermal and electrical conductivity, creating a

powerful vortex. This closely aligns with modern concepts of Magnetohydrodynamics (MHD) or reactionless drives, which use magnetic fields to propel a craft without expelling mass.

2. Zero-Point Energy: The sheer, impossible capability of these craft to defy gravity and traverse vast distances points to an energy source that taps into the quantum fabric of space—zero-point energy—a clean, abundant power source that remains theoretical in modern physics, yet seems to have been engineered by the ancients.

Advanced Materials Reacquisition:

The Engineered Loss

The loss of key materials science underscores the abrupt end of the curriculum:

- Damascus Steel and Nanomaterials: The legendary properties of Damascus Steel, known for its strength, flexibility, and distinct surface patterning, were lost after the 18th century. Modern analysis has revealed the presence of carbon nanotubes and cementite nanowires in the ancient steel—a complex microstructure achievable only through meticulous, long-lost metallurgical processes involving specific raw materials and thermal cycling. The existence of ancient nanotechnology in the form of superior metal alloys proves that an entire, advanced materials science was purposefully allowed to atrophy.

Today, the most ambitious and classified government projects are dedicated to achieving the propulsion systems and material science the ancients took for granted, confirming that we are simply following the original, aborted blueprint.

SECTION III.

BIO-ENGINEERING AND THE CHRONOLOGICAL RETRACTION

The greatest proof of the external agency's ability to manage technology is their mastery of biological science—a power directly reflected in the textual alterations that created our short, constrained human lifespan.

The Genetic Constraint:

Imposing the Human Operating System

The pre-flood genealogies documented in texts globally, including the Book of Genesis, record unnaturally long human lifespans (e.g., Methuselah at 969 years). After the major intervention (the Flood, the Tower of Babel, or the ancient conflicts), this longevity immediately and abruptly decreases, dropping to 120 years or less.

This is not a failure of myth; it is the fingerprint of genetic management. The advanced agencies possessed the technology not just for physical engineering, but for biological engineering, setting a maximum potential lifespan for the human species. Thus, retraction of the Managed Curriculum included the imposition of a genetic filter—a deliberate shortening of the human operating cycle to prevent the accumulation of too much knowledge over generations, thus ensuring the continued control of the new, simplified religious narrative.

Modern Biophysical Re-Awakening

Our modern technology is now confirming this ancient capacity to manage life at a foundational level:

1. **CRISPR Technology:** The invention of CRISPR has given humanity the ability to edit the human genome with unprecedented precision. We are now capable of targeting specific DNA sequences to cure disease and, theoretically, extend life. This is the exact capacity that the external agencies demonstrated when they genetically constrained the human species millennia ago.

2. **Water Memory and Cellular Consciousness:** Modern biophysics research increasingly points to the idea that biological systems, including water and cellular structures, hold a form of non-DNA-based memory. The abrupt, global decline in human longevity suggests the external agency

may have engineered a biophysical limitation—a command structure outside of DNA—that governed the human operating system's maximum runtime. Our modern medical breakthrough is merely the laborious re-acquisition of a tool that was used against us in the deepest past.

The convergence is clear. The "lost science" of the ancients—manipulating matter with sound, harnessing extraordinary energy, and controlling the biological clock—is identical to the goal of our most innovative, 21st-century physics and biology. We are simply following the original, aborted blueprint.

Chapter 9:
The Integrated Hypothesis:

When Deep Time Meets Scripture

The Foundation of Logical Consistency

The biblical narrative insists that humanity's history began approximately 6,000 years ago with the singular creation of Adam and Eve. This premise serves as the Supernatural Answer's fundamental anchor. Yet, as established in the preceding chapters, this short timeline is directly and scientifically refuted by the vastness of Deep Time and the indisputable evidence of human antiquity. This chapter applies the analytical consistency of the Humanistic Initiative to integrate established scientific truths—the Big Bang, Evolution, and the archaeological record—into a cohesive framework, showing that the Scientific/Extraterrestrial Answer provides the most logically consistent explanation for our history.

SECTION I.

THE CHRONOLOGICAL COLLAPSE AND COSMIC ARCHEOLOGY

The 6,000-year timeline collapses instantly under archaeological scrutiny. This is not a matter of subtle dating error; it is a chronological chasm between scientific fact and religious doctrine.

The 315,000-Year Barrier

In 2017, the discovery of Jebel Irhoud remains in Morocco pushed the timeline for Homo sapiens back to an astonishing 315,000 years ago. These modern human forms existed 311,000 years before the biblical date of creation. Further remains in Ethiopia have been dated to at least 233,000 years ago. These are irrefutable facts that demand a non-literal interpretation of scripture.

This deep time is governed by the principles of cosmic evolution. The universe's immense age of 13.8 billion years, confirmed by definitive evidence that galaxies are receding from one another (Hubble's Law), established the conditions for life itself. The laws of physics, once set in motion by the Big Bang, ensured that, given the right chemical conditions, organic molecules would form.

The Cosmic Architect vs. The Local Interventionist

This logic leads to an inescapable conclusion: the fundamental building blocks of life (the "Atoms," or ADAM, in a metaphorical sense) were scattered throughout the cosmos.

1. **Cosmic Architect:** This perspective does not inherently eliminate a Creator, but it redefines the Creator's role from a singular, local sculptor to a

Cosmic Architect who designed the physical laws that guarantee life's emergence across billions of galaxies.

2. **Local Interventionist:** This is the agency that found Earth—a functioning planet—and chose to manage or edit the emerging life forms. To maintain the belief that our small planet in one small solar system is the sole crucible for intelligent life is an act of extreme cosmic selfishness, defying all statistical probability established in Chapter Five.

SECTION II.

THE COGNITIVE UPGRADE:

SOLVING THE GREAT LEAP AND THE FERMI PARADOX

The archaeological record shows that early Homo sapiens existed in a state of relative stasis for hundreds of thousands of years, spending over 200,000 years simply perfecting basic hand-ax technology. This suggests the biological hardware was present, but the operating system was dormant.

The Great Leap Forward: Discontinuous Acceleration

Then, at some point between 70,000 and 40,000 years ago, the human species experienced a profound and unexplained cultural explosion often called the "Great Leap Forward." This event saw the sudden, unprecedented appearance of:

1. Abstract Cognition: Intentional burial rituals, symbolic art, and musical instruments.
2. Sophisticated Communication: Complex language with syntax capable of transmitting abstract ideas.
3. Technological Shift: Projectile weapons, fishing gear, and tailored clothing.

The magnitude of this shift is staggering: a species that took 200,000 years to move from a stone to a better stone suddenly began to master self-expression, mathematics, and complex social organization. This rapid, discontinuous acceleration defies the expected pace of Charles Darwin's theory of natural selection alone. We need an explanation for the sudden influx of superior intellectual capacity—a cognitive upgrade that enabled abstract thought and complex cultural transmission.

The Fermi Paradox Answer

The physicist Enrico Fermi posed the famous question: "Where is everybody?" Given the age of the universe and the statistical likelihood of widespread intelligent life, why have we found no evidence of them?

The Scientific/Extraterrestrial Answer provides the most compelling solution to both the Great Leap and the

Fermi Paradox: They were here, and their evidence is mislabeled as mythology. The sudden, dramatic increase in cognitive superiority, the unexplained appearance of technologies that later manifest in the religious "miracles" (Chapter 3), and the ability to organize the massive construction projects (Chapter 4) become logically reconcilable if a genetic or informational intervention occurred. The beings who came here did not stay because their mission was one of management, not cohabitation. The evidence of their presence remains in our biology and our lost technology.

SECTION III.

THE LOGIC OF ADVANCED TECHNOLOGY AND THE WEIGHT OF EVIDENCE

To discount the detailed accounts of advanced weaponry found in the ancient Sanskrit texts (Chapter 6)—like the Barbarika's Teen Baan (functionally identical to a modern guided missile system) or the Brahmastra (the effects of a thermonuclear weapon)—as mere mythology requires a complete sacrifice of logic.

The logic is reversed: These stories exist because the events occurred. The people who witnessed them described advanced devices—flying machines, weapons of enormous destructive capability, and genetic manipulation—using the only language they possessed: that of Gods, magic, and demons.

The logical conclusion is this: The rapid acceleration of Homo sapiens was caused by an external force that imparted knowledge and possibly genetic material. This intervention—the extraterrestrial hypothesis—serves as the missing explanatory variable that solves the historical, archaeological, and biological riddles left unanswered by traditional theology or slow-paced evolution.

SECTION IV.

THE HUMANISTIC CHOICE: CONSISTENCY VERSUS COMFORT

The final choice in this exercise of Comparative Speculation rests with the individual reader, but the Humanistic Initiative demands that this choice be made with intellectual consistency.

When presented with a profound historical puzzle, a rational mind must choose the explanation that accounts for the maximum amount of verified data with the minimum amount of logical contradiction.

In the words of the age-old saying: **If it walks like a duck, and talks like a duck, it must be a duck.** When an undeniable pattern of technological intervention looks like the genetic acceleration of a species and solves the paradoxes of history, yet we refuse to acknowledge it as the most logical explanation, we are sacrificing rational consistency for emotional comfort.

The evidence presented throughout this work compels the hypothesis that: **The vastness of the cosmos guaranteed the emergence of intelligent life elsewhere, and the abrupt acceleration of human history suggests that life found us, providing the technological and genetic components that our primitive minds interpreted as divinity.**

The chains of forced belief are broken not by a new dogma, but by the application of unyielding logic. The truth will set you free, but only if you are willing to face the facts, regardless of where they lead you.

Chapter 10:
A Shared Destiny:

The Humanistic Future

The New Mandate

The goal of The Humanistic Initiative was not to eliminate faith, but to conduct an exercise in Comparative Speculation—to reveal which explanation for human origins is most logically consistent with the verifiable scientific and archaeological record. We have established that the Supernatural Answer, reliant on a singular, recent creation event, collapses under the weight of Deep Time and internal contradictions. Conversely, the Scientific/Extraterrestrial Answer provides the missing explanatory variable for rapid genetic acceleration, anomalous technology, and the universal narratives of "Gods" who descended from the heavens.

The evidence presented throughout this work compels a single, profound philosophical conclusion: the human race has been governed, constrained, and intellectually limited by narratives that were deliberately shortened, moralized, and enforced. To claim our rightful place in the cosmos, we must first break the historical chains of this forced belief and embrace the Humanistic Initiative—the pursuit of truth through unyielding reason, logical consistency, and a profound commitment to human potential.

SECTION I.

THE CATASTROPHIC COST OF EXCLUSIVITY AND DOGMA

The greatest moral indictment against the Supernatural Answer is not its lack of scientific proof, but its historical reliance on coercion and violence to maintain ideological consistency. The moment a religion claims exclusivity—that it, and only it, holds the singular, non-negotiable path to eternal truth creates an ethical mandate for the elimination of dissent.

The Historical Record of Atrocity

The annals of history are tragically replete with examples of powerful religious factions enforcing conformity through brutal acts. This pattern proves that fear, not enlightenment, has been the foundational tool of faith maintenance:

1. The Spanish Inquisition (1478–1834): This systematic campaign to maintain Catholic orthodoxy across the Spanish kingdoms resulted in an estimated 150,000 investigations. While historians debate the final execution count, the threat of torture and the auto-da-fé (public act of

faith) enforced a terrifying psychological control that eliminated intellectual freedom for centuries.

2. The Crusades (1095–1291): This series of religiously motivated wars, primarily against Muslims and other "non-believers," demonstrated that the pursuit of sacred land and adherence to a prescribed faith were considered more valuable than human life. The historical cost is measured in millions of lives and the destruction of cultural centers like Constantinople in the Fourth Crusade.

3. The Suppression of Science: The persecution of figures like Galileo Galilei (for supporting the heliocentric model) and the systematic destruction of non-conforming knowledge—such as the burning of the Library of Alexandria—demonstrate a consistent, institutional hostility toward objective, verifiable truth.

Morality that must be enforced through violence is not divinely perfect; it is human control disguised as piety. A truly divine, all-powerful creator would have no need for human agents to murder, torture, or coerce belief; its truth would be self-evident, universal, and non-negotiable to all rational minds. The documented history of forced conformity serves as the final ethical proof that reliance on singular, unprovable dogma leads directly to human atrocity.

SECTION II.

THE ARCHITECTURAL FRAUD:

THE GREAT OBFUSCATION

Our investigation into world history revealed a timeline where the most primitive human understanding was centered not on a singular, recent creator, but on "Star Beings" and powerful entities from the heavens. The beliefs of the Sumerians, Egyptians, and countless indigenous cultures—documented in writings that long predate the formalization of Judaism and Abrahamic traditions—are focused on physical, powerful entities who interacted directly with humanity, gifted them knowledge, and built the magnificent structures we now debate.

The Toba Catastrophe and the Genetic Bottleneck

The Great Obfuscation was the process by which this clear, primordial truth was gradually replaced by the short, moralizing narrative of the modern religions. This was necessitated by geological and biological trauma.

1. The Toba Catastrophe Theory posits that a super volcanic eruption in Sumatra approximately 75,000 years ago caused a massive global cooling event, leading to a profound genetic bottleneck. Human population may have plummeted to a few

85

thousand individuals globally. This event would have effectively reset human technological and cultural memory.

2. The Great Leap Forward (Chapter 8) occurring 40,000 to 70,000 years ago, directly following the Toba event, is perfectly consistent with a re-intervention by the external agencies to restore the human line, followed by the implantation of the "cognitive upgrade."

The core of this obfuscation was the reduction of time. By anchoring creation to a mere 6,000 years ago, the 315,000 years of human existence—the vast window of time that allowed for multiple interventions, genetic alterations, and re-acquisitions of technology—was erased. The purpose was simple: To remove humanity's history is to remove its potential. If we are told we are only 6,000 years old, we cannot conceive of the 315,000-year-old Star Beings as our mentors; we can only view them as Gods who demand unquestioning submission.

SECTION III.

THE CERTAINTY OF UNCERTAINTY:

THE NEW COSMIC MANDATE

Our journey has led us to the certainty that neither the divine Creator nor the extraterrestrial Creator can be proven with current empirical evidence. The pursuit of truth has revealed an ultimate void: we have no definitive, verifiable knowledge of our fate after death. Since the most fundamental questions remain empirically unproven, the ethical focus must shift entirely to verifiable human action, in the here and now.

The Liberation of Cognitive Dissonance

The ultimate power of the Humanistic Initiative lies in the acceptance of this uncertainty. It frees the mind from the shackles of fear—the fear of a vengeful God, the fear of an eternal hell—which have been used for millennia to suppress inquiry.

1. Cognitive Dissonance: To maintain the 6,000-year timeline, the mind must actively reject overwhelming geological and archaeological data. This mental friction drains cognitive resources. By accepting the full 300,000-year history, the mind achieves logical consistency, freeing up all intellectual capacity for creation and discovery.
2. The Kardashev Scale: The Russian astrophysicist Nikolai Kardashev proposed a scale to measure a civilization's level of technological advancement based on its energy usage. A Type I civilization can harness all the energy available on its home planet. The Humanistic Future demands we prioritize the scientific, zero-point energy goals that will advance us to Type I status, preparing us for the cosmic community, rather than remaining chained to the tribal conflicts of a primitive past.

By choosing reason over dogma, we choose to prioritize: Life over Doctrine, Consistency over Comfort, and Potential over History.

SECTION IV.

THE NEW HUMAN AGENDA: RECLAIMING OUR DESTINY

The most staggering paradox revealed by this work is the unmatched engineering of the past—the mercury of Teotihuacan, the impossible precision of Baalbek, the genetic leap forward—followed by the extended period of stagnant intellectual dark ages that coincided with the enforcement of exclusionary religious dogma. The moment we put a book in front of us and declared it the final word, we ceased writing our own history.

The Humanistic Future demands a new agenda, one that reclaims the scientific potential of our managed past:

1. Re-acquisition of Zero-Point Energy (ZPE): We must recognize that our pursuit of clean, anti-gravity propulsion is not a new exploration. The principles of ZPE are encoded in the descriptions of the Vedic Mercury Vortex Engines (MHD) and the physics required to move the megalithic structures of Baalbek. Modern physics confirms the potential: the Casimir Effect proves that energy exists in a vacuum, which is the foundational principle of ZPE. We must

aggressively fund and de-classify research into reactionless drives, demanding transparency regarding recovered anomalous materials (such as those associated with Element 115).

2. Global, Non-Exclusive Ethics (The Prime Directive): We must build a universal ethical framework based on rational, humanistic principles—one that would be applicable to the extraterrestrial community we will eventually join or encounter. This framework must value logic, verifiable truth, and the preservation of sentient life above all else, thereby ensuring we do not meet any future "Star Beings" with the same murderous exclusivity we showed our own kind. This means abandoning all exclusionary religious codes.

3. Unfettered Creation and Biometric Freedom: We must reclaim the biological potential that was constrained during the Great Obfuscation. Research into longevity, genetic editing (CRISPR), and materials science (nanotechnology, self-healing compounds) should be prioritized. Imagine what we could create if the vast wealth, energy, and mental resources currently expended on defending contradictory dogmas were instead dedicated to scientific exploration and social advancement.

The Humanistic Initiative is not a plea for atheism; it is a mandate for maturity. We have demonstrated that the scientific evidence—the missing 315,000 years, the technological anomalies, the statistical certainty of life elsewhere—is overwhelmingly consistent with a history of external, advanced intervention. Whether a distant, divine Creator set the Big Bang in motion is a question we cannot answer. But whether we allow human fear and manufactured scripture to continue to block our intellectual growth is a choice we make every day.

The most consistent truth is that the answers to our history lie not in a short, exclusive book, but in the boundless, ancient, and beautiful cosmos. Our destiny is a shared destiny, and it is time for humanity to reclaim the full potential of its incredible, 315,000-year-old mind.

CHAPTER 11:
THE HUMANISTIC INITIATIVE:

THE HUMANISTIC BLUEPRINT:

A MANIFESTO FOR RECLAIMED DESTINY

The Humanistic Initiative is no longer a philosophical hypothesis; it is the inevitable conclusion drawn from the verified, 317,032-year history of our species. We have proven the Chronological Lie was a political fabrication, a tool of social and intellectual control designed to enforce Technological Amnesia. Our final task is not to discuss the merits of the evidence—those are settled—but to define the immediate, actionable blueprint for dismantling the infrastructure of the Lie and accelerating humanity into its rightful place as a Type I civilization.

SECTION I.

THE INFRASTRUCTURE OF THE LIE: UNMASKING THE GATEKEEPERS

The "Fabrication of the Fence" (Chapter 9) is not maintained by ancient parchment alone; it is upheld by highly organized, contemporary institutions that suppress the full, 315,000-year record of human potential. To reclaim our destiny, we must identify and bypass these gatekeepers.

The Educational Mandate: Replacing Dogma with Data

The current global educational model—the initial layer of the fence—prioritizes standardized obedience and historical sanitization. We must institute the Historical Correction.

1. Actionable Step: Every curriculum must teach the full 315,000 TRE, beginning with the archaeological fact of Jebel Irhoud, not the 6,000-year fiction.
2. Outcome: By presenting anomalous technology (the Antikythera Mechanism, the Baghdad Battery) as a standard part of ancient history, we restore the expectation of superior past knowledge, eliminating the intellectual concept of "primitive man."

The Financial and Political Gate: The Cost of Denial

The most immediate cost of the Supernatural Answer is the colossal misallocation of global resources.

1. Religious Economy: Billions of dollars in annual, tax-exempt revenue are funneled into defending exclusionary dogma, maintaining real estate portfolios, and funding conflicts rooted in sectarian division. This capital, which is generated by the cognitive dissonance of the

population, is a massive drain on scientific progress.

2. Political Inertia: Political systems are paralyzed by dogma-driven conflicts (e.g., resource wars justified by faith, opposition to genetic research). The Humanistic Initiative demands the Reclamation of the Public Purse: Redirecting tax-exempt revenue from dogmatic institutions toward verifiable, scientific pursuits, such as zero-point energy and global climate solutions.

SECTION II.

THE POST-THEOLOGICAL ECONOMIC MANDATE: REDIRECTING WASTED CAPITAL

The economic reality of a post-theological world is one of unparalleled potential. The energy currently wasted on defending an unprovable concept must be redirected to re-acquiring the proven technology of our managed past.

The Zero-Point Energy (ZPE) Mandate

Our greatest technological loss was the ability to harness limitless, non-polluting energy—the technology that powered the Vimanas and moved the stones of Baalbek. This science is now being slowly, painfully re-acquired under different names.

1. The Blueprint: We must immediately elevate research into Magnetohydrodynamics (MHD) and

reactionless drives, viewing the Vedic texts and descriptions of the Ark's power system not as mythology, but as an advanced engineering specification.

2. Quantified Goal: The Humanistic Initiative targets the full, demonstrable, commercial viability of ZPE within the next 50 years. This timeline is achievable once the vast, tax-exempt capital and mental resources currently locked up by the infrastructure of the Lie are freed and aggressively directed toward this singular goal.

The Bio-Sovereignty and Longevity Mandate

The retraction of the Managed Curriculum led to the immediate and artificial shortening of the human lifespan (Chapter 7).

1. Actionable Step: Full, unfettered support for CRISPR and genetic longevity research, viewing the 900-year lifespans recorded in the pre-Flood genealogies as achievable genetic potential, not miraculous fiction.
2. Ethical Foundation: The moral authority for genetic manipulation is solely derived from the human species, not from edited texts that mandate constraint. This shift eliminates the dogma-driven delays that currently plague bio-engineering progress, rapidly accelerating our species toward genetic self-determination.

SECTION III.

THE REACQUISITION TIMELINE: FROM TYPE 0 TO TYPE I

The Kardashev Scale defines our ascent. Humanity is currently a fragmented, volatile Type 0 Civilization, relying on inefficient chemical combustion. The Humanistic Initiative sets the goal of achieving full Type I status—mastering all energy available on Earth—within the next century.

This timeline represents the absolute minimum potential for a species operating with Logical Consistency—a species no longer spending its energy fighting ghosts from its own edited past.

SECTION IV.

THE UNEDITED HUMAN: RECLAIMING GENETIC DESTINY

The Humanistic Initiative is the final, grand act of self-reclamation. It is the end of intellectual dependency. We must stop defining our destiny by the constraints of a book written by Bronze Age political agents. Our true nature is encoded not in scripture, but in the 315,000-year-old genetic blueprint left behind by the Ancient Intelligence—a blueprint that was edited but not destroyed.

1. The choice is now simple and binary: Remain a Managed Species: Continue to allow our lives to be governed by the fears, taboos, and false timelines of the Supernatural Answer, perpetually remaining a volatile, technologically constrained Type 0 civilization.
2. Become the Sovereign Species: Embrace the full scientific reality of our past, redirecting all resources and mental capital toward ZPE, genetic mastery, and interstellar capability.

The evidence is the key, and the truth of our past is the path to our unified future. The Movement begins now; with the knowledge you hold. Let us together take the next step forward!

MAY ALL WHO LIVE BE WELL AND FIND ENLIGHTENMENT IN ALL THEY DO.

Select Bibliography (APA 7th Edition)

The following works represent the core scientific, archaeological, and historical texts that informed the comparative speculation and ultimate hypothesis of this volume, presented in compliance with the APA 7th Edition citation standard.

I. Scientific & Archaeological Timeline (Deep Time and Cosmology)

1.   Dalrymple, G. B. (1991). The age of the earth. Stanford University Press.

2.   Hublin, J. J., et al. (2017). New Jebel Irhoud hominin finds and the origin of Homo sapiens. Nature, 546(7657), 289–292.

3.   Lemaitre, G. (1950). The primeval atom: An essay on cosmogony. D. Van Nostrand Company.

4.   White, T. D., et al. (2003). Pleistocene Homo sapiens from Middle Awash, Ethiopia. Nature, 423(6941), 742–747.

II. Ancient Engineering & Artifacts (Megaliths and Anomalous Technology)

5.   Gómez Chávez, S., & Heilen, R. B. (2014). The Tlaloc an project: Archaeological investigations in the

tunnel under the Pyramid of the Feathered Serpent, Teotihuacan. Ancient Mesoamerica, 25(2), 467–483.

6.   Hancock, G. (1995). Fingerprints of the gods: The evidence of Earth's lost civilization. Crown Publishers.

7.   König, W. (1938). Ein galvanisches Element Aus der Zeit der Parther [A Galvanic Element from the Parthian Period]. Forschungen und Fortschritt, 14(1), 8–9.

8.   Schoch, R. M. (1998). Voices of the rocks: A scientist looks at catastrophes and ancient civilizations. Inner Traditions/Bear & Company.

III. Scripture, Mythology, and Comparative Religion

9.   Chadwick, H. (1967). The early church. Penguin Books.

10.   Kramer, S. N. (1961). Sumerian mythology: A study of spiritual and literary achievement in the Third Millennium B.C. University of Pennsylvania Press.

11.   Monier-Williams, M. (1899). A Sanskrit-English dictionary: Etymologically and philologically arranged. Oxford University Press.

12.   Peters, E. (1988). Inquisition. University of California Press.

13.   Temple, R. K. G. (1998). The Sirius mystery: New scientific evidence of alien contact 25 years later. Inner Traditions.

IV. Genetic & Evolutionary Theory

14.   Mellars, P. (2005). Why did the Homo sapiens 'Great Leap Forward' occur and why was it concentrated in Africa? Evolutionary Anthropology: Issues, News, and Reviews, 14(2), 49–60.

15.   Oppenheimer, S. (2004). Out of Africa's Eden: The people of the world. Carroll & Graf Publishers.

V. Extraterrestrial/Suppressed Technology

16.   Good, T. (1988). Above top secret: The worldwide U.F.O. cover-up. William Morrow.

17.   Oganessian, Yu. Ts., et al. (2004). Experiments on the synthesis of Element 115 in the Am-243 + Ca-48 reaction. Physical Review C, 70(6), 064608.

Epilogue:

The Cost of Waiting

We have journeyed together through deep time, traversing epochs where a 6,000-year narrative shrinks to a momentary flicker. We have confronted archaeological inconsistencies, examined the high-tech anomalies left by the ancients, and traced the political lines drawn to enforce singular dogma. The inquiry is complete, but the work is just beginning.

This book was not an attempt to replace one faith with another. It was a call to intellectual maturity. The greatest ethical failure of our civilization has not been the mistakes we have made, but the comfortable consistency of our inquiry failures—the continuous willingness to sacrifice verifiable evidence for emotional security. We chose the simple, singular answer over the complex, integrated truth.

The central realization is this: The most profound miracle is not an event occurring once in a single location, witnessed by a few, and defying all known laws of physics. The most profound miracle is the continuity of life itself over the span of 300,000 years. It is the complex, layered, and often messy process of evolution, intervention, loss, and rediscovery that defines our species.

The Integrated Hypothesis is not a final destination, but a starting gun. It demands that we transition from a reactive species, waiting for a savior or a divine blueprint, to a proactive species, reclaiming our agency and preparing for our inevitable destiny in the cosmos. If our history were managed, our future would be deliberate.

The cost of waiting—waiting for clarity from on high, waiting for an accepted authority to give permission to think—is the cost of sacrificing our future. The truth, as we have seen, is not supernatural; it is archaeological, written in the stone, the stars, and the very structure of our DNA. The responsibility now lies with the 300,000-year-old mind to finally interpret that record correctly and move forward.

Acknowledgements

This book, The Humanistic Initiative, is the culmination of a lifelong quest for consistency, a journey that could not have been completed without a foundation of unwavering love and support.

My deepest gratitude belongs to my wife Misty. You believed in my quest, and more importantly, you believed in me, providing not just logistical support but the steady, calm presence that made it all possible. Thank you for your unwavering faith in me.

To my children — Izzy, Tristian, Jayce, Dylan, and Kirstin you are the reason I grapple with complex questions of morality and ethics. You are the genesis of my hope and the ultimate inspiration for the humanistic outlook this book champions. Your futures are the greatest argument for pursuing truth without fear.

Finally, I wish to acknowledge the brave intellectual pioneers who gave me the courage, the inspiration, and the initial foundation to put these thoughts on paper. Your tireless work in challenging established narratives and exploring the unexamined corners of history and the cosmos is the true spark of comparative speculation. I am profoundly grateful for the dedicated research and thought-provoking analysis shared by:

- Dr. Michio Kaku

- Giorgio A. Tsoukalos

- David Childress

- William Henry

- Erich von Däniken

- Linda Moulton Howe

- Nick Pope

- George Noory

- Travis S. Taylor

Thank you to every reader, every family member, and every skeptic whose questioning mind helped shape the pages of this book.

About the Author

William Bowden began his life without a map, moving constantly between states from South Carolina to Louisiana. This lack of steady roots—coupled with years spent working a myriad of jobs and engaging with people from every corner of the globe—became his greatest strength, training him to question every received piece of wisdom. His lifelong motto remains: "Believe half of what you see and none of what you hear."

William is a technical expert extensively trained in welding, metallurgy, materials process, and design. This professional drive to uncover the truth of materials—how they are constructed, how they fail, and what their composition reveals—became the engine for this book's intellectual mission.

Having pursued formal education later in life, he brings a unique blend of scientific rigor and grounded skepticism to the greatest mysteries of human history. As a husband and father of six, and a grandfather, the question of humanity's true origins is not academic, but deeply personal. He wrote The Humanistic Initiative to provide a logical framework for a shared, optimistic cosmic future.

THE TRUTH IS NOT SUPERNATURAL. IT'S ARCHAEOLOGICAL.

For millennia, humanity has anchored its sense of purpose and morality to a 6,000-year timeline—a narrative of singular creation and divine exclusivity. But what happens to that story when 300,000-year-old human remains are unearthed in Morocco? What if the "miracles" of scripture were simply advanced technology witnessed by primitive minds?

In The Humanistic Initiative, author William Bowden Jr issues a radical challenge, moving beyond belief to engage in Comparative Speculation. This is not a book about proving aliens; it is a rigorous, fact-based investigation into which hypothesis—the Supernatural Answer or the Scientific Answer—is most logically consistent with the evidence we can actually verify.

You will confront the uncomfortable truths science reveals:

- The Logical Collapse: Why the Trinity is a manufactured political decree, how the biblical timeline is shattered by Deep Time, and why the history of forced religious conformity is the ultimate ethical failure of exclusivity.

- The Global Signposts: The staggering proof that the ancient world mastered physics and chemistry impossible for the time—from the Baghdad Battery and the Teotihuacan mercury to the Sirius B knowledge of the Dogon people.

•	The Integrated Hypothesis: How the abrupt "Great Leap Forward" in human evolution is best explained by a Managed Curriculum—a genetic intervention that accelerated our species and left us a legacy of high-tech artifacts and mythological cover stories.

The Humanistic Initiative is a manifesto for intellectual maturity. It demands that we abandon the comfort of singular dogma and the fear of the unknown to embrace the complexity of our history. The choice is clear: Do we continue to sacrifice rational consistency for emotional comfort, or do we reclaim our 300,000-year-old mind and prepare for our inevitable destiny in the cosmos?

The fate of humanity depends on the consistency of this inquiry.

www.ingramcontent.com/pod-product-compliance
Lightning Source LLC
Chambersburg PA
CBHW051105250726

48656CB00001B/491